THE BEST OF
MEXICO

THE BEST OF
MEXICO
A COOKBOOK

Evie Righter

Recipes by Kathi J. Long
Food photography by Steven Mark Needham

CollinsPublishersSanFrancisco
A Division of HarperCollinsPublishers

First published in USA 1992 by CollinsPublishersSanFrancisco

Produced by Smallwood and Stewart, Inc.
New York City

© 1992 Smallwood and Stewart, Inc.

Edited by Alice Wong
Jacket design: Nina Ovryn   Book design: Dianna Russo
Food styling: Ann Disrude   Prop styling: Betty Alfenito
Recipe consultant: Gloria Soto

Photography credits: E. R. Degginger/Picture Perfect: 43; 81.
Karen Nelson: 7. Galen Rowell/Mountain Light: 57. Tim Thompson: 72.
Stuart Wasserman/Picture Perfect: 10; 85. Nik Wheeler: 1; 2-3; 19.

Library of Congress Cataloging-in-Publication Data

Righter, Evie
    The Best of Mexico: a cookbook/Evie Righter;
recipes by Kathi J. Long.
    p. cm.
    Includes index.
    ISBN 0-00-255148-9
    1. Cookery, Mexican.   I. Title.
TX716.M4R49   1992
641.5972—dc20   92-19622
                                          CIP

Printed in China

8 10 9

Contents

Introduction

Every cuisine in the world is rooted in history. And while volumes have been written about Mexico's past, it is only recently that the cuisine of this dramatic, vibrant country has been chronicled for its extraordinary complexity and diversity, and for its marvelous melding of different cultures and distinct regions. This is a cuisine that has had to adapt, but one that remains remarkably intact. It is spirited; it is strong; it is from the ground up. Its beginnings are ancient.

Geography has been a harsh master of what grows in Mexico. The sun is unforgiving. The days are long and hot. Much of the land is simply not arable. Thousands of years ago, before Christ, it was discovered that corn ~ *maíz* ~ would grow, and grow plentifully. Great Indian civilizations ~ the Olmec, Maya, Toltec ~ learned how to grow corn, roast it, grind it, and cook with it. They even learned to trade with it. Farming became a way of life for these diverse, often warring cultures. Each of these empires ultimately would rise and fall, but the

A candy store on the Cinco de Mayo, Mexico City

presence of corn as a way of life prevailed. Added to this was the discovery that beans and *chiles* ~ hot peppers ~ of all types could be grown and cultivated, and that like corn, beans and *chiles* could be dried, and the basis of Mexican cooking was established.

The Aztec empire, which followed that of the Toltecs and flourished from the 1400s on, became the last great Indian empire of Mexico. In the late 1400s, Spanish explorers in search of the fabled spice routes of India made landfall in Cuba, and it was from there in 1519 that Hernán Cortés set sail and landed on the coast of the Gulf of Mexico in what is now Veracruz. It is fair to say that nothing in Mexico was ever the same. It would take Cortés two years to conquer the Aztec emperor Montezuma II and his incredible capital of Tenochtitlán, just north of Mexico City, but conquer Cortés did.

The vicissitudes of colonialism in general have been well documented over time. In Mexico, as in so many other captured lands, good came with the bad. The Spanish, recognizing that fortunes could be made in this vast, untapped country, remained and transplanted their folkways to the strange land they called New Spain. They brought with them their way of life, including food from their homeland ~ pigs, cattle, wheat, olives. These ingredients would find their way into the very fabric of everyday Mexican cooking, whose dishes had put corn, tomatoes, beans, squash, nuts, seafood, even chocolate to such succulent use. The Spanish also brought rice, which thrives in certain areas of Mexico and has established itself as the second most important grain, after corn.

It is the pig, though, that dramatically changed the cooking of Mexico. Before the arrival of the Spanish, the diet of the Mexican Indian had been basically vegetarian. Now the pleasures of cooking with pork would be explored, and the Indians began to use the pig in every conceivable culinary way. This legacy is evident even today in the predominance of lard as a cooking fat.

But there is still something more. While the conquistadors may have been able to subdue the land under one rule, they could not have a consonant effect on the cuisine. From region to region and state to state, certain dishes, made with ingredients available in one specific area only, remained decidedly distinct, and today are celebrated as classics. Thus do you have the seven great *moles,* or sauces, of the state of Oaxaca. Similarly, Puebla is known the world over for its turkey in a *chile* and chocolate sauce, or *mole poblano.* Another great dish of Mexico, *pozole,* or hominy stew, is made either with red sauce, spicy and hot from dried red *chiles,* or green sauce, fragrant with fresh green *chiles* and herbs, depending upon where you are. There is also

Metates and manos used for grinding

everyday cooking and *fiesta*, or party, dishes, such as *tamales*, and no two regional *tamal* recipes are ever the same. Simple, wonderful seafood preparations on the Gulf, Caribbean, and Pacific coasts abound. In the north, where wheat is grown, wheat-flour tortillas prevail over the staple corn tortilla so favored in its infinite adaptability in central and south Mexico. Use of *chiles* is determined by which ones grow where. Beans, however, are the staff of life in Mexico, and know no regional boundaries.

The intriguing subtleties and splendid diversity of Mexican cooking can only be touched upon in a collection such as this one - forty-six recipes in all. If what we have imparted, though, is the flavor and spirit of this wonderful sunny, dynamic cuisine, rich with the twists and turns of history, then that is a successful start. We leave it to you to pursue all that remains.

Evie Righter

Agua de Melon & Enchiladas Suizas, page 56

AGUA DE MELON

Melon Water

As anyone who has been to Mexico knows, the sun there is hot. Whether
you are in the highlands or on the coast, in the noise of Mexico City or in a
quiet village, relief can come in different ways ~ few more refreshing than the one
below. A variation on an ade, this fruit-flavored water is frequently sold from stands
on the streets and in the open-air markets. Other fruits, like watermelon or
strawberries, can be substituted.

*Two 2½-pound ripe
cantaloupes*

5 cups cold water

*¼ cup plus 3 tablespoons
superfine sugar, or to taste*

Ice cubes or cracked ice

Cut each melon in half, scoop out and discard the seeds. Remove the rind and cut melon into 1-inch cubes. In a blender or food processor blend half the melon with ½ cup water until smooth. Repeat with the remaining melon and ½ cup water. Transfer the purée to a pitcher and add the remaining 4 cups water and the sugar, to taste. Stir until the sugar is dissolved. Transfer into a large pitcher and pour into glasses filled with ice. Makes about 12 cups.

MARGARITAS

Orange Margarita and Gold Margarita

In Mexico, tequila is drunk straight by the jigger. If you are not up to tequila full strength, we offer two tequila-based drinks below. Theory has it that *margaritas* were actually invented State-side, but their popularity seems to know no bounds.

ORANGE MARGARITA

2½ tablespoons white tequila

1 tablespoon Triple Sec

½ cup fresh orange juice

2 tablespoons fresh lime or lemon juice

1 teaspoon superfine sugar

Coarse salt

Ice cubes or cracked ice

Slice of lime for garnish

In a cocktail shaker or blender, combine well the tequila, Triple Sec, orange juice, lime juice, and sugar.

Moisten the rim of a glass with water, then dip it in the salt to coat. Fill glass with ice and pour mixture over it. Garnish with lime. Makes one 8½-ounce drink.

GOLD MARGARITA

3 tablespoons gold tequila

1 tablespoon plus 1 teaspoon Triple Sec

4 tablespoons fresh lime juice

1 tablespoon superfine sugar

Coarse salt

Ice cubes or cracked ice

Slice of lime for garnish

In a cocktail shaker or blender, combine well the tequila, Triple Sec, lime juice, and sugar.

Moisten the rim of a glass with water, then dip it in the salt to coat. Fill glass with ice and pour mixture over it. Garnish with lime. Makes one 8½-ounce drink.

CAFÉ DE OLLA

This classic preparation for spiced coffee is popular throughout Mexico. *Served after dinner, dessert, or, if desired, at breakfast, the brew is very aromatic and sweet. Authentically, the coffee would be served in earthenware mugs. The olla of the Mexican recipe title refers to the earthenware pot in which this coffee has traditionally been made.*

4 cups water

⅓ cup packed dark brown sugar

One 3-inch piece cinnamon stick

8 whole cloves

One 3-inch piece orange peel, pith removed

½ cup coarsely ground dark-roasted coffee

Milk or cream, if desired

In a saucepan over medium-high heat, combine the water, sugar, cinnamon stick, cloves, and orange peel and bring mixture to a boil, stirring occasionally. Reduce to low heat to a bare simmer and let mixture steep covered for 5 minutes. Remove saucepan from heat, stir in the coffee, and let it steep covered for 8 minutes. Strain coffee through a sieve lined with cheesecloth into a warm coffee pot and serve immediately with milk or cream, if desired. Makes 4 cups.

Champurrado & Buñuelos, page 87

CHAMPURRADO

Hot Chocolate Atole

The haunting aroma of cinnamon makes itself known in any number of Mexican dishes, from entrées to desserts. Here, and in the preceding recipe, it is used to scent a hot beverage. While the addition of *masa harina* to hot chocolate may surprise some, the result affects the texture of the drink favorably, rendering it not as pourable as regular coffee nor as dense as porridge, but somewhere in between, gruel ~ and hence, its name *atole*, which actually means gruel. And the flavor of the *masa harina* is subtly recognizable as well. This is a classic combination from Oaxaca.

⅓ cup masa harina

1½ cups water

One 5-inch stick canela *or three 2-inch sticks cinnamon*

½ cup packed dark brown sugar

2 cups milk

1 cup heavy cream

One 3-ounce tablet Mexican chocolate or 2 ounces extra-bittersweet chocolate, chopped

1 teaspoon pure vanilla extract

In a heavy saucepan combine the *masa harina* and the water, stirring until smooth. Add the *canela* and cook over medium-high heat about 8 to 10 minutes, or until thickened, whisking constantly. Add the sugar, milk, cream, and chocolate and stir to combine well.

Bring mixture to a boil over medium-high heat, then simmer uncovered over low heat for about 5 minutes, stirring occasionally. Stir in vanilla extract. Strain and discard solids and serve immediately. Makes 5 cups.

SALSA DE JITOMATE COCIDA

Chili-Tomato Sauce

The renowned *salsas* of Mexico add spirit and spark to whatever they accompany. The variations are many, but *salsas* usually have four ingredients in common: tomatoes, *chiles,* onions, and garlic. This basic combination can be served uncooked, cooked, or even roasted and then puréed coarse. The sauce here should be simmered to the thickness of spaghetti sauce and will enliven a simple grilled fish or *Huevos Rancheros* (p. 33). To maximize the rich flavor of cumin, *comino* in Spanish, dry-toast the seeds in a skillet, then grind finely in a spice or coffee grinder.

Two 28-ounce cans whole
Italian plum tomatoes, plus
juice

⅓ cup vegetable oil

1¾ cups chopped white onions

2 teaspoons minced garlic

3 small bay leaves

1 tablespoon dried oregano

2 to 3 chiles de árbol, *crushed,*
or 2 teaspoons crushed red
pepper flakes

1½ teaspoons freshly ground
toasted cumin

Chicken Stock (p. 36), if
needed

Salt to taste

In a food processor pulse half the tomatoes with juice 8 to 10 times until coarsely puréed. Repeat with remaining tomatoes. Set aside.

Heat oil in a saucepan over medium-high heat and cook the onions and garlic, stirring frequently, for 2 to 3 minutes, or until softened. Add the bay leaves, oregano, *chiles,* cumin, and tomatoes, and stir to combine. Reduce heat to low and simmer gently, stirring frequently, for 35 to 45 minutes, or until thickened. If sauce becomes too dry, add stock to thin. Salt to taste. Let cool. Covered and chilled, sauce will keep 1 week. Makes 6 to 7 cups.

An outdoor market in San Miquel de Allende

SALSA VERDE

Tomatillo Sauce

Picante, or spicy, describes this flavorful sauce of fresh ingredients ~ *tomatillos, chiles,* onions, and garlic ~ that are roasted for richness, puréed, then combined with a bold measure of pungent *cilantro.* When buying *tomatillos,* look for those that are bright green and hard to the touch, not yellow or soft. While this *salsa verde* was created essentially as a sauce to be served with tortilla chips, it is also very good as a garnish on chicken, fish, or meat dishes.

1½ pounds tomatillos, *husked & rinsed*

1¼ cups chopped white onions

4 large garlic cloves, peeled

3 or 4 chiles jalapeños, *stemmed, to taste*

3 tablespoons vegetable oil

1 teaspoon coarse salt, or to taste

½ teaspoon freshly ground black pepper

½ cup coarsely chopped cilantro

Preheat the oven to 450°F. In a bowl toss together the *tomatillos,* onions, garlic, *chiles,* oil, salt, and pepper. Transfer the mixture to a small baking pan and roast for 45 minutes. Remove from oven and let cool.

In a food processor pulse the *tomatillo* mixture until coarsely processed. Add *cilantro* and more salt, if desired, and pulse 3 or 4 times to combine. Covered and chilled, the sauce will keep up to 3 days. Makes 3½ cups.

GUACAMOLE

Avocado Dip with Tomato and Fresh Chilies

Avocados, without which there wouldn't even be *guacamole* ~ and what
a loss that would be! ~ are said by some to have been brought to Mexico from
Ecuador by the Incas in the fifteenth century, and there is evidence that *guacamole*
itself is a centuries-old preparation. Debate continues about how textured
guacamole should be. Some say it should be chunky; others say it should be smooth.
One thing is certain: For this very popular, what amounts to a world-class dip, use
avocados ripened to that perfect point of readiness. Of the avocados available in the
States, we recommend the Haas variety with its nubbly skin and dark color,
because of its buttery texture and rich flavor. Beyond that, the remaining
ingredients must be the freshest ones possible.

*2 ripe Haas avocados, about 8
    ounces each*

½ cup diced white onion

½ cup diced plum tomatoes

2 tablespoons finely chopped
chile serrano

⅓ cup coarsely chopped cilantro

1 tablespoon fresh lime juice

*1½ teaspoons coarse salt, or
    to taste*

Close to serving time, cut each avocado in half and remove the pit. Score each half into ¼-inch cubes with the tip of a small sharp knife. Scoop the avocado cubes into a bowl and coarsely mash them with a fork. Add the onion, tomatoes, *chile*, *cilantro*, juice, and salt, and combine. Keep covered with plastic wrap until ready to serve. Makes 2½ cups.

PICO DE GALLO

Mexican Salsa

Among the many *salsas* and condiments in Mexican cooking, *pico de gallo*
is a favorite and is prepared throughout the country in any number of different
ways. Whatever its ingredients, here are the unsullied tastes of tomatoes, avocado,
and *chiles* ~ a usual but never wearing triumvirate. The relish can be relied upon to
perk up tortilla chips or serve as a garnish for *Carne Asada* (p. 67) or other roasted
meats, poultry, or fish. As to the difference in appearance between *chiles serranos* and
jalapeños, the *serranos* are tapered and about 1½-inches long and ½-inch wide; the
jalapeños are slightly darker in color and longer as well. Both are hot fresh *chiles*. For
less of their fiery effect, remove both the seeds and the ribs, wherein much of the
power of the pepper resides. To do so, wear gloves and be
sure not to touch your eyes. Then chop the peppers.

½ Haas avocado, pitted

2 cups chopped plum tomatoes

½ cup chopped white onion

¼ cup to ⅓ cup finely chopped
chiles serranos *or* chiles
jalapeños

⅓ cup coarsely chopped cilantro

2 tablespoons fresh lime juice

3 tablespoons juice from chiles
jalapeños en escabeche

1 teaspoon coarse salt, or to taste

Score avocado half into ¼-inch cubes with the tip of a sharp knife. Scoop avocado cubes into a bowl. Add the tomatoes, onion, *chiles*, *cilantro*, lime juice, and *chile* juice, and combine. Salt to taste. Let stand at room temperature for 10 minutes for flavors to blend. Makes 3 cups.

Pico de Gallo & Guacamole, page 21

23

CEBOLLAS EN ESCABECHE

Pickled Onions

For this zesty garnish, or snack, you want the reddest red onions you can find and an inexpensive jug-type red wine vinegar. A more expensive, aged, dark vinegar will tint the onions an unappealing brown. The color should be a heavenly pink; the flavor only slightly pickled, essentially sweet. In Mexico, there are different renditions of this recipe; this one is unique and modern-day in its use of juice concentrate, which lends an appealing, full, orange flavor. Use as a topping on any soft taco, especially ones with pork, with *Camarones Asado al Achiote* (p. 74), or as an accompaniment to a green salad. Note: You will need two days to complete the pickling process.

5 cups red wine vinegar

1 cup frozen orange juice concentrate, thawed

1½ cups superfine sugar

3 tablespoons coarse salt

1 tablespoon dried oregano

½ cup vegetable oil

2 pounds medium red onions, peeled & slivered

Combine all the ingredients except the onions in a large bowl and stir until the sugar is dissolved. Add onions and combine well. Cover bowl and let onions stand overnight at room temperature.

The following day, stir the mixture, then refrigerate, covered. Pickled onions will keep, covered and refrigerated, for at least 1 month. Makes 6 to 7 cups.

TOTOPOS

Tortilla Chips

No one needs to be reminded of the incredible popularity of Mexico's
tortilla chip or, for that matter, all that accompanies it. They are addictive when
served with a spicy *salsa* for dipping (pp. 18~22) and make the perfect
match for a salt-rimmed *Margarita* (p. 14). Several points to remember
when making them: Be sure that the oil is heated to the proper temperature;
watch them as they cook, and remove them almost before the bubbling stops
or they will quickly overbrown; and, lastly but importantly, serve them warm,
which brings out the tantalizing flavor of corn.

12 corn tortillas
Vegetable oil for frying
Salt, if desired

Cut each tortilla into 6 wedges and spread on a baking sheet to dry at room temperature for several hours.

Heat about 1 inch of oil in a skillet over high heat to 375°F. Fry tortillas, in batches, for about 1½ minutes, or until the bubbling has nearly stopped and chips are crisp and golden. With a slotted spoon transfer to paper towels to drain. Salt if desired and serve warm. Can be stored in an airtight container. Reheat in a 350°F. oven for 8 to 10 minutes. Makes 6 dozen.

CEVICHE DE HUACHINANGO

Marinated Red Snapper Cocktail

In Mexico there are different variations on the basic theme of *ceviche* ~ fish or shellfish "cooked" by the acid in fresh citrus juice. In this popular version, red snapper fillets are marinated in lemon and lime juices overnight, and then tossed with tomato, *chiles*, and herbs for a crisp and delicious result. Begin with the freshest fish available and marinate it no longer than twelve hours, or the fish will become mealy. This is a wonderful first course for a hot summer evening meal.

1½ pounds boneless red snapper fillets, skinned & cut into ½-inch cubes

1 cup fresh lemon juice

1 cup fresh lime juice

1 tablespoon dried oregano

1 tomato, cut into ¼-inch dice, about 1 cup

2 red onions, cut into ¼-inch dice, about 1 cup

2 to 4 tablespoons finely chopped chiles serranos, *to taste*

½ cup coarsely chopped cilantro

¼ cup coarsely chopped fresh mint, if desired

⅓ cup thinly sliced celery

½ cup fresh orange juice

1 teaspoon coarse salt

⅓ cup julienned radish for garnish

Check the fish for bones, then combine with lemon and lime juices and oregano in a non-aluminum container, and stir gently. Cover with plastic wrap and refrigerate overnight, but no more than 12 hours.

Drain the fish and transfer to a bowl.

Add the remaining ingredients, except the radish, and combine well. Let the *ceviche* stand at room temperature for 10 minutes. Adjust seasoning. Serve *ceviche* on salad plates or in small bowls and garnish each serving with some of the radish. Serves 6.

EMPANADAS CON HONGOS

Empanadas with Mushrooms

The *empanada* is a Mexican turnover made with a tender pastry. They can have either a sweet or savory filling and some are fried, like the ones below, while others are baked. Here we use mushrooms ~ a vegetable well liked in Mexico ~ with fresh *chiles* and *epazote* for a simple and fresh-tasting filling. If fresh *epazote* is not available, use *cilantro*, a herb totally different in flavor, but just as wonderful paired with mushrooms. Turn the *empanadas* carefully when frying and serve them immediately as an hors d'oeuvre or as part of a light buffet.

2 cups all-purpose flour

2 teaspoons coarse salt

3 tablespoons lard or vegetable shortening

1 egg yolk

½ cup ice water

3 tablespoons vegetable oil, plus additional for frying

2 cups slivered white onions

1 teaspoon minced garlic

6 ounces mushrooms, stemmed & thinly sliced

4 chiles jalapeños, *stemmed, seeded, ribbed, & thinly sliced lengthwise*

¼ cup coarsely chopped fresh epazote, *or* ¼ cup coarsely chopped cilantro

¼ teaspoon freshly ground black pepper

In a large bowl, combine flour and 1 teaspoon salt, and cut in lard until mixture resembles the texture of coarse cornmeal. In a bowl, beat the egg yolk with water and add to flour mixture. Mix with a fork until it forms a ball. Knead dough for about 5 minutes, or until smooth and elastic. Divide and shape into 12 small balls, about the size of golf balls. Cover with a damp cloth and let rest for 1 hour.

Heat 3 tablespoons oil in a skillet over medium-high heat and sauté the onions and

garlic for about 3 minutes, or until softened. Add the mushrooms and sauté for about 5 minutes, or until mushrooms start to release moisture. Add the *chiles, epazote* or *cilantro*, remaining 1 teaspoon salt, and pepper and stir to combine well. Remove from the heat and let cool.

On a lightly floured surface, roll each ball of dough into a 3-inch circle with a rolling pin, and cover with cloth.

Spread 2 tablespoons of mushroom filling over the bottom half of each dough circle and brush the edges with a bit of water. Fold circle in half over filling and press the edges together with tines of a fork to seal. Cover with a cloth.

Heat about 1½-inch of oil in a skillet over medium-high heat to 375°F. Fry the empanadas, 2 or 3 at a time, for 2 to 3 minutes per side, or until golden. Transfer to paper towels to drain. Keep warm in a 200°F. oven until ready to serve. Makes 12 empanadas.

TAMALES CON PUERCO Y CHILE ROJO

Tamales with Pork and Red Chili

It is interesting that *tamales,* filled and wrapped in corn husks or banana leaves and looking for all the world like small packages, were actually offered as gifts to the gods during the twelfth month of the eighteen-month-long Aztec year. To this day, *tamales* are still considered *fiesta,* or party, food, and, depending where you are in Mexico, they can have any number of different fillings. The ones below derive from Jalisco in the south of Mexico. Be organized before you embark upon making them. Check that the pot you intend to steam the *tamales* in is large enough, and replenish it with water over the course of steaming. The outer wrapping of aluminum foil here is for convenience; remove it before serving.

One 8-ounce package dried corn husks

12 chiles guajillos, *stemmed, or to taste*

2 pounds boneless pork butt, cut into ½-inch cubes

8 cups water

1½ cups lard or vegetable shortening

2 teaspoons minced garlic

6 tablespoons plus 2½ cups masa harina

1 tablespoon plus 1½ teaspoons coarse salt

1 teaspoon baking powder

16 pieces aluminum foil, cut in 12- by 10¾-inch pieces

Soak the corn husks in boiling water to cover for 30 minutes. Drain.

In a bowl, weigh down and soak the *chiles* in 2 to 3 cups of boiling water for 30 minutes, or until softened. Transfer *chiles* to a blender

with 1 cup soaking liquid and purée until smooth and thick. Add more soaking liquid if needed. Strain to remove solids.

In a medium saucepan over high heat, add the pork and 6 cups water, and bring to a boil.

Reduce the heat and simmer gently for 20 minutes. Remove pork and reserve the cooking liquid.

Heat ½ cup lard in a skillet over medium-high heat. Add the pork and cook, stirring, 10 to 12 minutes, or until browned. Add the garlic, 6 tablespoons *masa harina*, 1½ teaspoons salt, and the remaining 2 cups water, and stir to combine well. Stir in the *chile* purée, bring the mixture to a boil, and reduce the heat. Simmer for 5 minutes, stirring frequently. Set the filling aside.

Heat the remaining 1 cup lard in a saucepan over medium-high heat. In a large bowl combine the baking powder with the remaining 2½ cups *masa harina* and salt, then slowly whisk in 2 cups of the reserved pork stock until the mixture is lump-free. Whisk in the hot lard until the mixture is smooth and thick, but still spreadable.

Put 1 piece of foil on a work surface and place 2 pieces of the corn husks in the center of the foil, side by side, overlapping 1 inch.

Place ⅓ cup of the *masa* mixture in the center of the husks and flatten to a 2- by 3-inch square. Place about 3 tablespoons of the filling down the center of the *masa*. Fold the foil and corn husk over the *masa* and filling, so that the *masa* partially covers the filling, and continue folding to the end of the foil. Fold the bottom of foil and corn husk up and the top down into a 1½- by 3-inch rectangle. Repeat to make 16 tamales.

Stand the tamales side by side in a metal steamer and steam, covered, for about 1½ hours. Check the water level in the steamer about every 10 minutes, adding more boiling water if necessary. To check for doneness, remove 1 tamale and open it. The *masa* should come away easily from the husk and be cooked through and not too sticky. Serve hot or at room temperature. Can be stored in the refrigerator for one week, or in the freezer. Reheat in a 350°F. oven for 30 minutes, or steam for 15 to 20 minutes. Makes 16 tamales.

HUEVOS RANCHEROS

Fried Eggs on Corn Tortillas with Chili-Tomato Sauce

You see this famous classic Mexican dish also called eggs country-style, ranch-style, or even farm-style. Clearly the combination originated from the days of the cattle ranch and cowhand, when a substantial mid-morning meal was needed after a cattle drive beginning at dawn. Serve *huevos rancheros* for breakfast or for brunch and accompany them with refried beans, the typical pairing.

Vegetable oil for frying, plus additional 1 tablespoon

4 corn tortillas

4 large eggs

2 cups Chile-Tomato Sauce (p. 18), heated

2 teaspoons coarsely chopped cilantro

Heat ½ inch of oil in a skillet over medium-high heat. Add each tortilla and fry for 5 seconds, or until softened but not crisp. Transfer to paper towels to drain.

Heat 1 tablespoon of oil in a large skillet over medium-high heat and fry each egg, 2 to 3 minutes, sunny side up. Put a tortilla on each plate and top with a fried egg. Pour ½ cup of the chili-tomato sauce around the white of each egg and sprinkle *cilantro* over the top. Serves 4.

Chilaquiles & Frijoles Refritos, page 81

CHILAQUILES

Fried Tortilla Strips with Chili Sauce

Chilaquiles, one of the most renowned tortilla dishes of Mexico, is served in Mexico City for brunch, in Oaxaca for *almuerzo*, and in the home throughout the country for a light Sunday night meal. This recipe depends upon only a handful of ingredients ~ tortillas, of course, tomatoes, onion, *chiles*, garlic, and cheese. The result is saucy and spicy, tempered by a mild cheese.

1½ pounds plum tomatoes

1½ cups chopped white onions

2 garlic cloves, peeled

12 chiles serranos, stemmed, or to taste

Vegetable oil for frying

12 corn tortillas, cut into strips ½ inch wide

Salt to taste

½ cup grated queso añejo or Monterey Jack cheese

Preheat the broiler. Broil the tomatoes, onions, garlic, and *chiles* in a baking dish 4 inches from the heat for 2 to 3 minutes, or until browned. Turn the vegetables over and broil for 2 to 3 minutes, or until browned. Let cool and peel tomatoes and *chiles*. Transfer vegetables in batches to a food processor and pulse until coarsely puréed.

Heat ½ inch oil in a skillet over medium-high heat to 375°F. Fry tortilla strips in batches for about 1½ minutes, or until slightly crisp and golden. Transfer to paper towels to drain.

Carefully remove all but 3 tablespoons of the oil in the skillet and heat over medium-high heat. Add the purée and the tortillas and stir gently to combine. Season with salt and heat for 5 to 7 mintues, or until the tortillas are heated through but still crisp. Sprinkle with the cheese and serve. Serves 6.

CALDO DE POLLO

Chicken Stock

Here is the foundation of many a Mexican recipe, especially soup. The stock's flavor is pure, its color golden. Fresh herbs, always preferred, do make a difference, but dried herbs can be substituted.

3 tablespoons vegetable oil

1½ cups chopped white onions

2 carrots, chopped

2 stalks celery, chopped

1 large head of garlic, unpeeled & cut in half horizontally

2 bay leaves

1 sprig fresh thyme or ¼ teaspoon dried

1 sprig fresh oregano or ¼ teaspoon dried

One 4-pound chicken or an equal amount in backs, necks, & wings

20 cups water

Heat the oil in a large 6-quart stockpot over medium-high heat, and sauté the onions, carrots, and celery, stirring, for 3 minutes. Add the garlic, bay leaves, and herbs, and place the chicken on top. Add the water and bring to a boil. Skim any scum. Reduce the heat to low and simmer uncovered for about 2½ to 3 hours. Remove the pot from the heat and strain the stock through a fine sieve lined with cheesecloth into a container. Let cool and refrigerate or freeze in small containers. Makes about 12 cups.

CALDO DE PESCADO

Fish Stock

A rich soup, like *Sopa de Mariscos* (p. 70), depends in large part on a full-bodied, perfumed fish stock as its base, and here is the perfect one. In Mexico, this recipe would not include the wine, added below for still more flavor and fragrance.

¼ cup vegetable oil

1½ cups chopped white onions

1 large head garlic, unpeeled & cut in half horizontally

4 stalks celery, chopped

2 large carrots, chopped

2 to 2½ pounds fish bones & fishheads, gills removed, & well rinsed

1 bunch fresh flat-leaf parsley

4 sprigs fresh oregano or 1 teaspoon dried

4 bay leaves

2 tablespoons white peppercorns

2 tablespoons whole coriander seeds

2 tablespoons whole allspice

2½ cups dry white wine

18 cups water

Heat the oil in a large 6-quart stockpot over medium-high heat, and sauté the onions, garlic, celery, and carrots for about 5 minutes. Add the remaining ingredients and stir to combine. Add water and bring to a boil. Skim any scum. Reduce heat to low and simmer uncovered for 1½ to 2 hours. Remove the pot from heat and strain stock through a fine sieve lined with cheesecloth into a container. Let cool and refrigerate or freeze in small containers. Makes about 12 cups.

SOPA DE LIMA

Lime Soup

There is a very, very tart, small, yellow lime that grows in the
Yucatán in Mexico, and if you are lucky enough to be there it will lend its distinctive
flavor to this soup. The juice from Persian limes is a reasonable substitute for that of
the Mexican *limones*; better yet, though, if you can secure them, begin with Key
limes from Florida. Don't even consider using leftover chicken here. This soup,
simple though it may seem, is a celebration of the purest, cleanest, loveliest flavors.

*¾ pound boneless, skinless
  chicken breast*

¾ cup diced plum tomatoes

¾ cup diced red onion

*2 tablespoons minced chile
  serrano or chile jalapeño*

*3 tablespoons coarsely chopped
  cilantro*

*6 to 8 cups Chicken Stock
  (p. 36), heated*

*¼ cup fresh lime juice, or to
  taste*

2 teaspoons coarse salt, or to taste

In a saucepan over high heat, add chicken and water to cover. Bring to a boil, reduce heat, and simmer covered for 15 minutes, or until tender. Let cool and shred.

Divide the chicken, tomatoes, onion, *chile*, and *cilantro* evenly among 6 bowls. Pour heated chicken stock into each bowl, then season to taste with lime juice and salt. Serves 6.

Sopa de Lima & Ensalada de Jícama, page 86

SOPA DE FRIJOLES NEGROS

Black Bean Soup

There are some cultures that rely heavily on a specific indigenous ingredient, or a handful of them, for sustenance of a very primal kind. In China, one has only to think of rice. In Mexico, the bean sustains. As is, beans are inexpensive and highly nutritional; and in combination with other specific food groups, they contribute their share to what some think healthwise is an almost perfect whole. This black bean soup calls for *chiles de árbol*, chicken stock, and herbs and spices for flavor and sophistication. If you can, by all means add the *epazote*, a traditional ingredient. If it is not available, this soup is still marvelously rich and spicy.

1 sprig fresh thyme or ¼ teaspoon dried

1 sprig fresh oregano or ¼ teaspoon dried

¼ ounce fresh epazote, if desired

¼ cup lard or vegetable oil

3 or 4 chiles de árbol, or 2 teaspoons red pepper flakes

1½ cups chopped white onions

2 teaspoons minced garlic

1 pound smoked pork shanks

½ teaspoon freshly ground toasted cumin (see p. 18)

½ teaspoon ground coriander

¼ teaspoon ground canela or ⅛ teaspoon ground cinnamon

Pinch of ground cloves

1 pound dried black beans, picked over & rinsed

8 cups Chicken Stock (p. 36)

2 or 3 tablespoons red wine vinegar or sherry vinegar

1 to 2 teaspoons coarse salt, or to taste

Slivered red onions for garnish

Tie the fresh herbs and *epazote*, if using, into a bundle with kitchen string. Melt the lard or heat the oil in a 4-quart saucepan over medium-high heat and sauté the *chiles* for 30

seconds, or until darkened but not burned. Add the white onions and garlic and sauté for about 3 minutes, or until softened. Add the pork and the herb bundle, or dried herbs if using. Stir in the spices, beans, and stock and combine well. Bring to a boil over medium-high heat, reduce heat, and simmer uncovered for 1¾ hours, stirring occasionally, or until the beans are soft. Add vinegar and salt and simmer soup for 30 minutes longer. Remove pork and herb bundle. Remove the *chiles* if desired. Serve in soup bowls and garnish with red onions. Serves 4 to 6.

SOPA DE ELOTE

Corn Soup

In the cooking of Mexico, one is continually witness to the extraordinary importance of corn in the diet. Here it is enjoyed in soup. There are more traditional recipes that use heavy cream as a means of smoothing the final texture and *masa harina* as a thickener. We have not used either, in favor of puréeing and sieving the soup base, to render it velvety smooth. Sometimes chopped fresh *chiles* are added; we have added *chipotle* purée, consistent with keeping the soup luxurious.

3 or 7 tablespoons vegetable oil

10 cups fresh corn kernels, about 14 ears, or frozen corn, thawed & dried with paper towels

2½ cups coarsely chopped white onions

2 large garlic cloves, peeled

4 cups milk

2 cups Chicken Stock (p. 36)

2 tablespoons Chipotle *Purée* (p. 70)

2 teaspoons coarse salt, or to taste

3 tablespoons coarsely chopped cilantro *for garnish*

If using fresh corn, heat 2 tablespoons of oil in a large skillet over medium-high heat and sauté half the corn for about 3 to 4 minutes, or until dark yellow. Transfer to a baking sheet to cool. Repeat with remaining fresh corn.

Clean out the skillet and heat 2 tablespoons oil. Sauté the onions for about 3 to 4 minutes, or until softened. Spread onions on a baking sheet and let cool. In the same skillet heat 1 tablespoon oil and sauté the garlic for 2 to 3 minutes, or until lightly browned. Add to the baking sheet and let cool.

In a blender purée ¼ of the fresh or frozen corn, onions, garlic, and 1 cup milk. Pour the purée through a medium-mesh sieve into a 3-quart saucepan, pressing the

Tarascan fishermen on Lake Pátzcuaro, Michoacán

mixture through with a rubber spatula. Repeat with the remaining corn, onions, garlic, and milk in batches.

Place the saucepan with the purée over medium heat, add stock, *chipotle* purée, and salt, and heat until hot but not boiling or it will curdle. Serve in soup bowls and garnish each serving with *cilantro*. Serves 6.

POZOLE ROJO

Hominy and Red Chili Stew

In Mexico there are red *pozoles*, like this one typical of the state of Jalisco, and green *pozoles*, vibrant with fresh herbs and green *chiles*. What each has in common is the dried slack corn ~ *pozole* ~ that uniquely identifies it. Otherwise known as hominy, it contributes remarkable texture, flavor, and perhaps, above all, character to this national dish. So favored throughout Mexico is this hearty stew that some restaurants there set aside their regular menus once a week in favor of *pozole* night. Serve *pozole* as a main course with just tortillas and a beverage ~ it needs little else.

1½ pounds dried white pozole

*4 sprigs fresh oregano or 1
    teaspoon dried*

*4 sprigs fresh marjoram or 1
    teaspoon dried*

*4 sprigs fresh thyme or 1
    teaspoon dried*

⅓ cup lard or vegetable oil

*1½ pounds boneless pork butt,
    cut into 1-inch cubes*

6 or 8 chiles de árbol, *stemmed,
    to taste*

*3½ cups coarsely chopped white
    onions*

8 large garlic cloves, peeled

2 large bay leaves

½ cup ground chile ancho

*1 pound smoked pork shanks,
    if desired*

16 cups beef stock

1 tablespoon coarse salt

Shredded cabbage for garnish

*Julienned strips of radishes for
    garnish*

Wedges of lime for garnish

In a large bowl soak the *pozole* in water to cover for 8 hours or overnight. Drain. Tie the fresh herbs into a bundle with kitchen string.

Melt the lard or heat the oil in a stockpot over medium-high heat, and cook the pork butt for 5 to 8 minutes, or until browned. Add the

chiles de árbol, and fry, stirring, for 5 to 10 seconds. Add the onions and garlic and sauté for 2 to 3 minutes, or until softened. Add the herb bundle, bay leaves, *chili ancho*, pork shanks, if using, *pozole*, and stock. If using the dried herbs, sprinkle into pot. Bring mixture to a boil, reduce heat, and simmer uncovered, stirring occasionally, for about 3 hours, or until the pork is tender and the *pozole* is puffed and chewy. Add salt and cook 5 minutes more. Remove and discard the herb bundle, *chiles de árbol*, bay leaves, and pork shanks. Serve the stew in soup bowls and garnish with cabbage, radishes, and lime. Salt to taste. Serves 8 to 10.

TORTILLAS DE MAÍZ

Corn Tortillas

Tortillas are the staff of life in Mexico, served for breakfast, lunch, and dinner, and at any other time during the day, in innumerable different ways. There are few Mexican preparations that don't presuppose a good supply of tortillas as an ingredient or an accompaniment. To make tortillas, you will need a tortilla press, available in cookware stores, and, to be authentic, a *comal* ~ a round baking sheet. A cast-iron skillet or griddle is a reasonable substitute.

2 cups masa harina

1 teaspoon coarse salt, or to taste

1 cup plus about 5 tablespoons lukewarm water

In a large bowl combine the *masa harina* and salt. Add 1 cup water and mix with your hands. Add remaining water, several tablespoons at a time as needed, until the dough forms a ball. Cover and let rest for 30 minutes.

Working with dampened hands, knead the dough for about 1 minute, then divide and shape into 12 small balls, about the size of golf balls. Keep covered with a damp cloth. Flatten each ball into a 5-inch circle between two sheets of plastic wrap on a tortilla press or with a rolling pin.

Heat an ungreased *comal* or iron skillet over medium-high heat. Peel top plastic from a tortilla and transfer, dough side down, to your hand. Peel plastic and gently place tortilla onto the hot *comal* or skillet. Cook for about 35 to 50 seconds per side, or until light brown bubbles are formed. Repeat with the remaining tortillas. Wrap in cloth and keep warm in a 150°F. oven until ready to serve. Can be stored wrapped in aluminum foil for several days in the refrigerator, or for a month in the freezer. Before serving, reheat on a hot skillet. Makes about 12 tortillas.

TORTILLAS DE HARINA

Wheat-Flour Tortillas

While the corn tortilla predominates in central and south Mexico, the wheat-flour tortilla prevails in the north, where the climate allows for wheat to grow. The mark of a well-made tortilla, corn or wheat-flour, is that it is pliable when cold. You know then that it can only become more yielding when warmed for serving. While we have frequently called for corn tortillas in the pages that follow, the wheat-flour tortilla is an equally good choice.

2 cups all-purpose flour
1½ teaspoons coarse salt
½ teaspoon baking powder

3 tablespoons lard
½ cup lukewarm water

In a large bowl combine the flour, salt, and baking powder. Cut in the lard, and add the water. Knead the dough for about 5 minutes, or until smooth and elastic. Cover and let rest for 30 minutes.

Knead the dough for about 1 minute, then divide and shape into 12 small balls, about the size of golf balls. Keep covered with a damp cloth. Flatten each ball into a 5-inch circle with a rolling pin.

Heat an ungreased *comal* or iron skillet over medium-high heat. Peel top plastic from a tor-tilla and transfer, dough side down, to your hand. Peel plastic and gently place tortilla onto the hot *comal* or skillet. Cook for about 35 to 50 seconds per side, or until light brown bubbles are formed. Repeat with the remaining tortillas. Wrap in a cloth and keep warm in a 150°F. oven until ready to serve. Can be stored wrapped in aluminum foil for several days in the refrigerator, or for a month in the freezer. Before serving, reheat on a hot skillet. Makes about 12 tortillas.

TACOS SUAVES DE POLLO

Soft Tacos with Chicken

Tacos suaves simply means soft tacos, and how delicious these filled tortillas can be! The filling may be simple and light, like the one below, or more sophisticated and spicy like the one on page 50. All you need to start is a supply of tortillas, then let your imagination be your culinary guide. Tacos are spontaneous and fun food. Beer and *Pico de Gallo* (p. 22) or *Salsa Verde* (p. 20) makes superb accompaniments.

¾ pound boneless, skinless chicken breast

Vegetable oil for frying

8 corn tortillas

½ cup slivered white onion

4 chiles jalapeños, stemmed, seeded, ribbed, & thinly sliced lengthwise

4 plum tomatoes, seeded & cut into ¼-inch dice

1 Haas avocado, peeled, pitted & cut into 8 slices

8 sprigs cilantro, about 4 inches long

2 limes, cut into 4 wedges each

Salt to taste

In a saucepan over high heat, add chicken and water to cover. Bring to a boil, reduce heat, and simmer covered for 10 to 15 minutes, or until tender. Let cool and shred.

Heat ½ inch oil in a skillet over medium-high heat to 375°F. Fry each tortilla for about 5 seconds, or until softened but not crisp. Transfer to paper towels to drain.

Spread about ¼ cup chicken over the bottom half of each tortilla. Sprinkle some onion, *chiles*, and tomatoes evenly over the chicken. Top with an avocado slice and a sprig of *cilantro*. Squeeze a wedge of lime over each filling and season with salt. Fold the tortillas in half and serve while still warm. Makes 8 tacos.

TACOS SUAVES CON PUERCO Y CHIPOTLES

Soft Tacos with Shredded Pork and Chipotles

There are *tacos suaves* with fillings as straightforward as simple
watercress sprigs drizzled with fresh lime juice and sprinkled with salt.
Then there is a combination like this one ~ tender pork and smoked *chiles*
on creamy refried beans, all encased in a delicately fried tortilla. A bit different,
very tasty, and proof that the variations for taco fillings can be limitless.

¾ pound boneless pork butt

*Vegetable oil for frying, plus
additional 4 tablespoons*

8 corn tortillas

*1 cup Refried Beans (p. 81),
heated*

*3 whole chiles chipotles en adobo,
thinly sliced, plus 1
tablespoon juice, or to taste*

½ cup slivered white onion

Salt to taste

*3 tablespoons coarsely chopped
cilantro*

In a saucepan over high heat, add pork and water to cover. Bring to a boil, reduce heat, and simmer covered for 40 minutes, or until tender. Let cool and shred.

Heat ½ inch vegetable oil in a skillet over medium-high heat to 375°F. Fry each tortilla for about 5 seconds, or until softened but not crisp. Transfer to paper towels to drain.

Heat 1 tablespoon oil in a skillet over medium-high heat. Add beans and *chile* juice and cook 1 to 2 minutes, or until heated through.

Heat the remaining 3 tablespoons oil in another skillet and sauté the onion for about 3 minutes, or until softened. Add *chiles* and pork and stir to combine well. Season with salt.

Tacos Suaves con Puerco y Chipotles & Tacos Suaves de Pollo, page 49

Spread 2 tablespoons beans over the bottom half of each tortilla. Divide the pork and *chile* mixture evenly over the beans, and garnish with *cilantro*. Fold the tortillas in half and serve while still warm. Makes 8 tacos.

Tostadas de Jaiba & Margarita, page 14

TOSTADAS DE JAIBA

Crab Tostadas

The words alone are beautiful ~ *taco, tostada, flauta* ~ and what each of these has in common is that it begins with that marvelous Mexican creation, the tortilla. The tostada is the tortilla fried, then topped. Here we use a unique crab salad ~ typical of one you might have in Veracruz. Serve these as a light summer lunch.

Vegetable oil for frying, plus additional ¼ cup

8 corn tortillas

1 cup slivered white onions

2 teaspoons minced garlic

¾ cup chopped ripe tomatoes

½ cup chopped green, unripe tomatoes

½ cup coarsely chopped cilantro

¼ cup coarsely chopped fresh flat-leaf parsley

⅓ cup chopped chiles jalapeños en escabeche, *plus ⅓ cup juice*

1 pound jumbo lump crabmeat, picked over for bits of cartilage & shell

Salt to taste

Pickled Onions (p. 24) for garnish

Heat ½ inch of vegetable oil in a skillet over medium-high heat to 375°F. Fry each tortilla for about 2 minutes, or until the bubbling stops and tortilla is crisp and golden. Transfer to paper towels to drain.

Heat the remaining ¼ cup oil in a skillet over medium-high heat and sauté the onions and garlic for about 3 minutes, or until softened.

In a large bowl combine the tomatoes, *cilantro*, parsley, *chiles*, juice, and crab. Add the onion mixture, salt, and combine well. Let the mixture stand for 10 minutes.

Top tortillas and serve immediately garnished with pickled onions. Makes 8 tostadas.

FLAUTAS CON CHORIZO, PAPAS, Y CHILES

Flautas with Sausage, Potatoes, and Chilies

Here we have Mexican flutes, as the word *flauta* suggests, but of the culinary kind, and they revolve around ~ once again ~ that most reliable round, the tortilla. Wrap them tightly for deep frying and serve them as soon as possible as they lose their crispness quickly. Again, the *chiles* here are optional, depending on your taste for spiciness. Serve with sour cream and *Guacamole* (p. 21).

12 ounces chorizo *or other spicy sausage, skinned & crumbled*

1 pound potatoes, peeled

3 tablespoons vegetable oil, plus additional for frying

¼ cup slivered white onion

2 teaspoons coarse salt

1 to 2 tablespoons Chipotle *Purée (p. 70), or 1 tablespoon plus 1 teaspoon chopped* chile chipotle en adobo, *plus 2 teaspoons juice, if desired*

12 corn tortillas

Sour cream and Pickled Onions (p. 24) for garnish

In a skillet over low heat, add the *chorizo* and cook, stirring occasionally, for 10 minutes, or until heated through. Drain thoroughly. Slice the potatoes ¼-inch thick, then into ¼ inch sticks.

Heat 3 tablespoons oil in a large skillet over medium-high heat and cook the potatoes, stir-ring frequently, for about 5 minutes, or until they begin to soften. Add the onion and the salt and cook, stirring frequently, for about 3 to 5 minutes, or until potatoes are softened. Remove from heat and stir in *chipotle* purée, or *chile* and juice, if using, and *chorizo*.

Preheat the oven to 350°F. Wrap tortillas

in aluminum foil and warm in the oven for about 15 minutes.

Spread about ¼ cup of *chorizo*-potato mixture down the center of a tortilla, roll tortilla up tightly, and secure with a toothpick. Repeat with remaining tortillas.

Heat ½ inch oil in a skillet over medium-high heat to 375°F. Fry the flautas, 2 at a time, for 2 to 3 minutes per side, or until crisp and golden. Transfer to paper towels to drain. Keep warm in a 200°F. oven until ready to serve. Remove toothpicks and top with sour cream and pickled onions. Makes 12 flautas.

ENCHILADAS SUIZAS

Enchiladas in Creamy Green Sauce

Enchiladas suizas are served throughout Mexico, favored for their
distinctive green sauce with cream. If you are lucky enough to find the Mexican
crema fresca, similar to sour cream but pourable and delicately flavored, by all means
use it. Otherwise, thick cream or crème fraîche is a good substitute.
Enchiladas suizas make a special, festive entrée.

½ *pound boneless, skinless*
chicken breasts

2 *tablespoons vegetable oil, plus*
additional for frying

⅓ *cup finely chopped white onion*

2 *teaspoons minced garlic*

¼ *cup finely chopped* chiles
serranos, *if desired*

3 *tablespoons coarsely chopped*
cilantro

1 *recipe* Salsa Verde *(p. 20)*

½ *cup thick cream or crème*
fraîche

Salt to taste

12 *corn tortillas*

½ *cup crumbled* queso añejo,
or crumbled feta cheese

In a saucepan over high heat, add chicken and water to cover. Bring to a boil, reduce heat, and simmer covered for 10 minutes, or until tender. Let cool and shred.

Heat 2 tablespoons oil in a skillet over medium-heat and sauté the onion and garlic for 3 minutes, or until softened. Add the *chiles,* if using, *cilantro,* and chicken, and stir to combine well. Remove from heat.

Heat the *salsa verde* in a saucepan over medium heat for 5 minutes. Stir in the cream and salt to taste. Keep sauce warm over low heat.

Preheat the oven to 350°F. Heat ½ inch oil in a skillet over medium-high heat to 375°F. Fry each tortilla for about 5 seconds, or

Puerto Escondido, Oaxaca

until softened but not crisp. Transfer to paper towels to drain.

Dip a tortilla into the sauce and transfer to a plate. Spread about 2 tablespoons filling down the center of the tortilla, then roll it up tightly. Transfer the enchilada, seam side down, to a 13- by 9- by 2-inch baking dish spread with 1 cup sauce on the bottom. Repeat with the remaining tortillas and arrange in one layer in the dish. Pour the remaining sauce over the enchiladas and cover with aluminum foil. Bake for about 20 minutes.

Remove the dish from the oven and remove the foil. Preheat the broiler. Sprinkle the enchiladas with the cheese. Broil 4 inches from the heat for 2 to 3 minutes to brown the top. Serves 6.

ENCHILADAS ROJAS CON QUESO

Red Enchiladas with Cheese

We have Oaxaca to thank for this renowned *enchilada* dish made red, savory, and spicy from *chiles guajillos*. The dried *guajillo* is pleasantly flavored, but is not fiery, and what heat it does render is moderated by the mild tasting *queso fresco*, or fresh cheese, of Mexico. The tortillas are dipped in *chile* sauce, stuffed, rolled, then true to their name ~ *enchilada* ~ covered with *chile,* again in the form of sauce.

21 chiles guajillos, *stemmed*

2 tablespoons white wine vinegar

1 teaspoon dried oregano

1 tablespoon sugar

Pinch of ground cloves

¼ teaspoon minced garlic

2 teaspoons coarse salt

3 tablespoons vegetable oil, plus
    additional for frying

12 corn tortillas

3¾ cups crumbled queso fresco,
    or grated Monterey Jack
    cheese

White onion rings for garnish

In a bowl, weigh down and soak the *chiles* in 4 cups boiling water for 30 minutes, or until softened. Transfer *chiles* to a blender with 1½ cups soaking liquid and purée until thick and smooth. Add more soaking liquid if needed. Strain to remove solids. Add the vinegar, oregano, sugar, cloves, garlic, and salt and stir to combine well.

Heat the 3 tablespoons oil in a saucepan

over medium-heat. Add the sauce and bring to a boil, stirring constantly. The sauce should be thick but pourable. If the sauce is too thick, add up to 1 cup water. Turn off the heat and let stand for 5 minutes.

Preheat the oven to 350°F. Heat ½ inch oil in a skillet over medium-high heat to 375°F. Fry each tortilla for about 5 seconds, or until softened but not crisp. Transfer to

paper towels to drain.

Dip a tortilla into the sauce and transfer to a plate. Spread ¼ cup cheese down the center of the tortilla, then roll it up tightly. Transfer the *enchilada,* seam side down, to a 13- by 9- by 2-inch baking dish spread with 1 cup sauce on the bottom. Repeat with the remaining tortillas and arrange in one layer into the dish. Pour the remaining sauce over the *enchiladas,* then sprinkle evenly with the remaining cheese. Bake for 20 minutes and serve garnished with onions. Serves 6.

POLLO EN PIPIÁN VERDE

Chicken in Pumpkin Seed Sauce

Oaxaca is credited with the creation of seven different but equally famous sauces, this one with green pumpkin seeds being among its most deservedly renowned. Nutty with peanuts and sesame seeds and complex with the flavors of two *chiles*, allspice and cloves, this sauce is remarkably light. *Tomatillos*, pumpkin seeds, lettuce, and herbs make it beautifully green. Serve this dish Mexican-style, with *arroz blanco*, white rice sautéed in oil with onion and garlic, then cooked in stock.

6 cups Chicken Stock (p. 36)

1½ cups chopped white onions

3 teaspoons coarse salt, or to taste

3 boneless, skinless chicken breasts, halved, about 2½ pounds

1½ cups pepitas *(unsalted, shelled pumpkin seeds)*

1 cup, about 5 ounces, dry-roasted unsalted peanuts

⅔ cup, about 4 ounces, sesame seeds

½ teaspoon freshly ground allspice

⅛ teaspoon ground cloves

½ teaspoon freshly ground black pepper

10 ounces tomatillos, *husked & rinsed*

1½ cups coarsely chopped white onions

2 large garlic cloves

2 medium chiles poblanos, *stemmed, seeded, & ribbed*

6 or 7 chiles serranos, *stemmed & chopped*

1 cup packed chopped Romaine lettuce leaves

2 cups coarsely chopped cilantro, *both stems & leaves*

1 cup coarsely chopped fresh flat-leaf parsely

8 tablespoons lard or vegetable oil

In a large saucepan over medium-high heat combine the stock, chopped onions, and 1 teaspoon salt, and bring to a boil. Add the chicken, reduce the heat to low, and simmer uncovered for about 8 minutes or until chicken is partially cooked. Remove pan from heat and let chicken cool in the stock. Reserve stock.

In an ungreased skillet over medium-high heat toast the *pepitas*, stirring constantly, for 3 to 4 minutes, or until they start to swell and the skins start to pop. Do not let seeds brown. Transfer to a plate. Toast the peanuts in the skillet, stirring constantly, for 2 to 4 minutes, or until slightly browned. Transfer to the plate with *pepitas*. Toast the sesame seeds in the skillet, stirring constantly, for 2 to 3 minutes, or until golden brown. Transfer to the plate with *pepitas* and peanuts.

In a food processor, add the seeds, peanuts, allspice, cloves, and pepper, and process for 20 to 30 seconds, or until finely ground. Transfer to a bowl. Add the *tomatillos*, coarsely chopped onions, and garlic to the work bowl and pulse 5 or 6 times. Add the *chiles*, lettuce, *cilantro*, and parsley, and pulse 10 to 12 times, or until blended but slightly grainy.

Heat the lard or oil in a large saucepan over medium-high heat, and cook the seed mixture, stirring constantly, for 4 minutes. Add 2½ cups of the reserved stock and the tomatillo mixture. Stir to combine well and cook for 15 minutes. Add the chicken, 2 cups reserved stock, and the remaining 2 teaspoons salt, and simmer uncovered for 10 to 15 minutes, or until the sauce is thickened but pourable. Add more stock if needed and salt to taste. Serves 6.

MOLE POBLANO DE GUAJOLOTE

Turkey in Chili-Chocolate Sauce

It is the sauce alone ~ the *mole* ~ of this great classic dish of Puebla that has made it world famous. Chili-based, with nuts, fruits, and chocolate added, the creation is credited to nuns, who, upon hearing that dignitaries, a bishop and a Spanish viceroy, were coming to the convent, prepared a dish worthy of such important guests. Exceptional is this dish and diners to this day applaud its uniqueness. Should the amount of lard, used as the cooking fat of Mexico, concern you, substitute olive oil ~ not typical, but more healthy. This recipe yields enough sauce to make this dish a second time. Store the sauce covered in the refrigerator for up to 5 days or freeze for up to 3 months.

½ pound lard

6 chiles anchos, stemmed, or to taste

6 chiles mulatos, stemmed, or to taste

8 chiles pasillas, stemmed, or to taste

4 ripe plum tomatoes

½ cup thickly sliced white onion

2 large garlic cloves, peeled

1 ripe plantain, peeled & sliced ½ inch thick

½ cup raisins

¼ cup plus 2 tablespoons sesame seeds, toasted (see p. 62)

½ cup dry roasted peanuts

2 ounces tortilla chips, about 1½ cups

¼ cup white wine vinegar

Three 3-ounce tablets Mexican chocolate or 6 ounces extra-bittersweet chocolate, chopped

Pinch of ground cloves

½ teaspoon freshly ground coriander seed

1 teaspoon ground canela or ½ teaspoon ground cinnamon

8 to 10 cups Chicken Stock (p. 36), heated

One 8-pound turkey or one 4- to 5-pound turkey breast

Salt to taste

Mole Poblano de Guajolote & Ensalada de Nopalitos, page 84

Heat the lard in a saucepan over medium-high heat. Add the *chiles* in batches and fry them for about 1 minute, or until puffed. Do not fry for too long or they will burn and be bitter. Transfer to a large bowl and soak, weighed down, in 4 to 5 cups boiling water for 1 hour, or until softened. Strain the lard into a bowl and reserve.

In a blender, purée the *chiles* and 1 to 3 cups of the soaking liquid, a small amount at a time, until smooth. The sauce should have the consistency of a slightly thick heavy cream. Strain to remove solids.

Preheat the broiler. Broil the tomatoes, onion, and garlic in a baking pan 4 inches from the heat for 2 to 3 minutes, or until browned. Turn vegetables over and broil for 2 to 3 minutes, or until browned. Let cool and peel tomatoes.

In a blender, combine in batches the vegetables, plaintain, raisins, ¼ cup sesame seeds, peanuts, tortilla chips, vinegar, chocolate, cloves, coriander, and *canela* with 2 cups stock. Purée until smooth.

Heat the reserved lard in a large saucepan over medium-high heat. Add *chile* purée and vegetable purée and whisk to combine well, taking care as mixture can splatter. Add 8 cups stock. Reduce to low heat and simmer uncovered, stirring frequently, for 1 hour, or until sauce is thick but pourable. Remove from heat and let stand at room temperature for 1½ hours. Cover and refrigerate overnight.

Preheat the oven to 350°F. Bake the turkey in a baking pan for about 1½ to 2 hours, or until tender. Let cool to room temperature, remove skin, and remove meat from the bones in whole pieces. Cut into ¼ inch slices, cover with plastic wrap.

Heat 7 cups sauce in a saucepan over medium heat. If sauce is too thick, thin it with warm stock. Add turkey and heat through. Serve on a platter and sprinkle with remaining 2 tablespoons sesame seeds for garnish. Serves 8 to 10.

Carne Asada & Sopa de Elote, page 42

CARNE ASADA

Grilled Steak

Grilling meat is an age-old preparation practiced the world over, but in few places has it been recognized in the same way as has *carne asada*, Mexico's great grilled steak. For the best results use skirt steak, the cut of choice, and marinate it simply, as directed below. Then sear it over hot coals outdoors. The outside will be slightly charred, the inside will be pink, the flavor will be superb. Serve with tortillas, *Guacamole* (p. 21), *Pico de Gallo* (p. 22), and perhaps grilled onions, also prepared over the fire. This is barbecue at its best.

1½ pounds skirt steak, cut into four equal pieces

2 tablespoons vegetable oil

2 teaspoons coarse salt

2 teaspoons freshly ground black pepper

2 limes, cut in half

Spread the meat on a work surface. Sprinkle 1 tablespoon oil, 1 teaspoon salt, and 1 teaspoon pepper, and squeeze juice from one lime over meat. Turn meat over and repeat. Let the meat marinate overnight.

Preheat a grill, or a heavy skillet, over medium-high heat. Add a piece of the meat and cook 2 to 4 minutes per side, or until medium-rare. Repeat with the remaining meat. Cut into thin slices, if desired, and serve immediately. Serves 4.

COSTILLAS EN SALSA VERDE

Pork Ribs in Green Sauce

Tomatillos, the basis of the green sauce that defines this dish,
also go by such names as *tomates verde*, green tomatoes, and husk tomatoes.
Indeed, *tomatillos* are lime-green in color, but are easily identified by the
parchment-like husk that encases them. In flavor, the fruit is lemony and acerbic,
but when roasted, puréed, and combined with *chiles, tomatillos*
provide a perfect counterpoint to the sweetness of pork. Serve
Mexican rice and refried beans with this dish.

1¼ pounds tomatillos, *husked &
rinsed*

1 large garlic clove, peeled

5 chiles de árbol, *stemmed*

1 cup water

3 pounds baby-back spareribs,
cut into single-rib portions

2 to 3 teaspoons coarse salt, or
to taste

3 to 6 tablespoons vegetable oil

⅓ cup chopped red onions
for garnish

⅓ cup coarsely chopped cilantro
for garnish

In a large skillet over high heat char the *tomatillos*, turning frequently, for about 3 minutes. Add the garlic and char, turning frequently, for about 2 minutes. Add the *chiles de árbol* and toast, turning frequently, for about 10 seconds. Transfer the contents into a blender, add the water, and process for 20 seconds, or until

puréed. Set green sauce aside.

Sprinkle the ribs with the salt. Heat 1 to 2 tablespoons of oil in a large skillet over medium-high heat and brown a third of the ribs, turning them, for about 6 to 7 minutes. Remove the ribs to a plate. Repeat with the remaining oil and ribs in batches.

Return all the ribs to the skillet. Pour

green sauce over ribs and simmer uncovered for 10 minutes, or until tender when pierced with a knife. Add salt to taste and cook 3 to 4 minutes longer. Transfer ribs and sauce to a platter and garnish with the onions and *cilantro*. Serves 4.

SOPA DE MARISCOS

Seafood Soup

Mexico's fish and shellfish dishes are justly famous and are as varied as the locales in which they are made. Here is an example of one of the more flavorful soups, with both spicy and smoky overtones, that puts the wealth of the waters to excellent use. Make the chili-tomato sauce in advance. Serve this soup as a main course with tortillas as an accompaniment, and *Ensalada de Jícama* (p. 83) as a side dish. *Flan* (p. 88) would be an appropriate and delicious ending to such a meal.

One 7-ounce can chiles chipotles en adobo

1 pound Manila clams, or other small hard-shelled clams

⅓ cup vegetable oil

1½ cups slivered white onions

2 teaspoons minced garlic

1½ pounds extra-large shrimp, about 18, shelled & deveined

18 oysters, shucked

1 pound squid with tentacles, cleaned, bodies cut into ¼-inch-wide slices

6 cups Fish Stock (p. 37), heated

2¼ cups Chili-Tomato Sauce, (p. 18)

⅓ cup coarsely chopped cilantro

2 teaspoons coarse salt, or to taste

2 cups cooked rice, hot

1½ limes, cut into 6 wedges

In a blender purée the *chiles* with their sauce. Strain to remove solids. Covered and chilled, the purée will keep for several months. Makes about ½ cup *Chipotle* Purée.

Rinse clams, and discard any that are open and do not close when touched.

In a 7-quart saucepan heat the oil over medium-high heat and sauté the onions and garlic for 2 minutes, or until softened.

Add shrimp and sauté for 1 minute. Add the clams, oysters, and squid, and sauté for 1 minute. Add 2 tablespoons *chipotle* purée, the stock, sauce, *cilantro*, and salt, and combine well. Cook the mixture covered for 3 to 4 minutes, or until the shellfish have opened.

Divide the rice among 6 large soup bowls. Arrange some shrimp, clams, oysters, and squid over the rice. Pour the stock with the onions and garlic over the shellfish. Garnish each serving with lime and serve immediately. Serves 6.

Sunrise at Copper Canyon, Chihuahua

CAMARONES CON AJO, CEBOLLAS, Y CHILES

Shrimp with Garlic, Onions, and Chilies

Along the coasts of Mexico seafood understandably dominates restaurant menus, and here is a dish that might well be served in the Yucatán or around the Gulf of Campeche. These shrimp are truly spicy with the combined flavors of two different kinds of *chiles*. *Chiles de árbol* are very hot. Begin with only one if you want to check the spiciness of the dish as you make it. Similarly, reduce the *chiles serranos* to taste. This dish is wonderful accompanied by *Arroz Mexicana* (p. 79).

5 tablespoons vegetable oil

2 cups slivered white onions

2 to 3 large garlic cloves, peeled & finely chopped

12 chiles serranos *or* chiles jalapeños, *stemmed, seeded, ribbed, & thinly sliced lengthwise, or to taste*

4 chiles de árbol, *stemmed & crushed,* or 1 to 3 teaspoons red pepper flakes

2 tablespoons unsalted butter

3 pounds extra-large shrimp, about 36, shelled & deveined

Heat 3 tablespoons oil in a large skillet over medium-high heat, and sauté the onions, garlic, and *chiles* for about 4 to 5 minutes, or until softened. Transfer to a bowl.

Clean the skillet and heat 1 tablespoon oil and 1 tablespoon butter over medium-high heat. Add half the shrimp, and brown for about 2 to 3 minutes per side, or until cooked through. Transfer to a plate. Repeat with the remaining oil, butter, and shrimp. Add the onion-*chile* mixture and all the shrimp, and stir to combine well for 1 to 2 minutes, or until the mixture is heated through. Serve immediately. Serves 6.

CAMARONES ASADO AL ACHIOTE

Grilled Achiote Shrimp

To make these exceptional marinated grilled shrimp on skewers, you will need *condimento de achiote*, a paste made from *annatto* seeds, ground *chiles*, and cumin, which is available in Latin or Hispanic markets. The *condimento* colors the shrimp a remarkable red-orange and flavors them with the distinctive appealing aroma of the *annatto* seed, a taste much appreciated in the Yucatán.

3 tablespoons vegetable oil

3 large garlic cloves, peeled

Three 4-ounce packages condimento de achiote, crumbled

3 tablespoons frozen orange juice concentrate, thawed

½ cup fresh grapefruit juice

1 tablespoon cider vinegar

3 tablespoons water

1 teaspoon freshly ground toasted cumin (see p. 18)

1 teaspoon freshly ground coriander seeds

1 teaspoon freshly ground canela or ½ teaspoon ground cinnamon

¼ teaspoon freshly ground cloves

½ teaspoon freshly ground black pepper

3 pounds extra-large shrimp, about 36, shelled & deveined

Mexican Rice (p. 79), heated

Pickled Onions (p. 24) for garnish

Heat oil in a skillet over medium-high heat and sauté the garlic, for 3 to 4 minutes, or until golden brown. Let cool and transfer garlic and oil to a food processor. Add the *condimento de achiote*, orange and grapefruit juice, vinegar, water, cumin, coriander, *canela*, cloves, and pepper, and process until smooth. Pour mixture into a large bowl, add the

shrimp, and stir to coat well. Cover and let shrimp marinate in the refrigerator overnight.

Preheat a grill or broiler with the rack 4 inches from the heat. Soak twelve 8-inch bamboo skewers in water for 20 minutes. Thread 3 shrimp through the middle on each skewer. Shrimp should form three "C" shapes in a row on each skewer. Grill or broil shrimp for about 2 minutes on each side, or until cooked through. Divide the rice among 6 serving plates and top with 1 or 2 skewers of shrimp. Garnish with pickled onions and serve. Serves 6.

PESCADO A LA VERACRUZANA

Red Snappper with Tomatoes, Onions, and Olives

A la Veracruzana ~ we have seen the phrase the world over, because this is a
world-class dish. From the city of Veracruz, this famous red snapper combination
marries the ingredients of Spain ~ olive oil, olives, capers, and assorted herbs ~ with
the ingredients of Mexico ~ *chiles*, tomatoes, and its unrivaled fresh fish. The
balance is unusually sublime; this is Mexican Gulf Coast cuisine at its very
finest. White rice and a salad are the perfect accompaniments.

*Six 8-ounce skinless & boneless
red snapper fillets, or other
mild-flavored white fish,
such as sea bass or striped
bass*

1½ limes, cut into 6 wedges

*2 to 3 teaspoons coarse salt, or
to taste*

2 teaspoons dried oregano

*One 28-ounce can whole Italian
plum tomatoes, plus juice*

½ cup vegetable oil

1 cup chopped white onions

1 teaspoons minced garlic

2 bay leaves

½ teaspoon dried thyme

½ teaspoon dried marjoram

1 teaspoon ground canela *or ½
teaspoon ground cinnamon*

Pinch of ground cloves

*36 small pimiento-stuffed olives,
rinsed & chopped*

*3 tablespoons large capers, rinsed
& chopped*

4 whole pickled chiles jalapeños,
*stemmed, seeded, ribbed, &
thinly sliced lengthwise, plus
¼ cup juice*

*1 cup Fish Stock (p. 37) or
Chicken Stock (p. 36)*

*Freshly ground black pepper to
taste*

*6 sprigs flat-leaf parsley for
garnish*

6 small chiles jalapeños *for
garnish*

Check the fish for bones. Arrange the fish in a single layer in a large dish and squeeze 1 lime wedge over each fillet. Sprinkle the fillets with the salt and oregano, cover with plastic wrap, and refrigerate for 30 minutes.

In a food processor pulse the tomatoes with juice 8 to 10 times, or until coarsely chopped. Transfer to a bowl.

Heat ¼ cup of oil in a large saucepan over medium-high heat and sauté the onions and garlic for about 3 minutes, or until softened. Add the bay leaves, thyme, marjoram, *canela*, and cloves and stir for 1 minute. Add the tomatoes and bring the mixture to a boil, stirring frequently. Reduce to low heat and simmer gently for 15 minutes. In a bowl, combine the olives and capers. Add half the olive mixture to tomato sauce, reserving the other half for garnish. Add the sliced *chiles*, juice, and stock to the pan and stir to combine well. Continue to simmer uncovered 20 to 30 minutes, or until slightly thickened and reduced to about 3 cups.

Preheat the oven to 375°F. Season the fillets with salt and pepper. Heat the remaining ¼ cup oil in a nonstick skillet over medium-high heat, and place two fillets, fleshy side down on the skillet. Cook for 3 to 4 minutes, or until golden brown. Turn over and transfer to a large baking dish, browned side up. Repeat with remaining fillets and arrange in one layer on the dish. Bake fillets for 5 to 7 minutes, or until cooked through and easily flaked with a fork. Add about ½ cup sauce to each serving plate. Top with a fillet, sprinkle with reserved olive mixture, and garnish with a parsley sprig and a whole *chile*. Serve immediately. Serves 6.

ARROZ MEXICANA

Rice with Tomatoes, Onion, and Garlic

One might suppose rice was indigenous to Mexico, so essential a food is it in the diet of the Mexican people. In fact, this grain was introduced to Mexico in the mid-sixteenth century, when it was embraced and quickly adopted. Among the *sopa secas,* or "dry soups" of Mexico, *arroz Mexicana* is one of the most famous, made throughout the country. Regional variations abound. In Puebla, green peas would be added. In Veracruz, look for plantains in the rice. And in Oaxaca, a region of remarkable cooking, there is a black rice, made with the cooking liquid of black beans.

¼ cup vegetable oil

1 pound long-grain white rice

1½ cups finely chopped white onions

1 teaspoon minced garlic

1 cup puréed whole plum tomatoes

3 cups Chicken Stock (p. 36)

2 teaspoons coarse salt

Heat the oil in a saucepan over medium-high heat and sauté the rice for about 5 minutes, or until opaque and just golden. Add the onions and garlic, and sauté for 2 minutes. Stir in the tomatoes, stock, and salt, and bring to a boil. Reduce heat to low, and simmer covered for about 25 minutes, or until all the broth has been absorbed. Remove from heat and let stand, covered, for about 5 minutes. Fluff rice with a fork and serve. Makes about 8 cups. Serves 6 to 8.

FRIJOLES

Beans

The bean is indigenous to Mexico, and on any given day, there is a pot
of them simmering slowly on the back burner of the stove in almost any
household. Beans are served for breakfast, lunch, and dinner. They are nourishing,
affordable, and adaptable to any number of variations. While black beans are more
typically served toward the interior of Mexico, pinto beans are the bean of choice
almost everywhere else. Some cooks will add *cilantro* to their beans; others, fresh
epazote to lend a pleasant, slightly acrid flavor to the sweetness of the beans.

¼ cup lard or vegetable oil

*1 medium white onion, unpeeled
& cut in half lengthwise*

*1 head of garlic, unpeeled &
cut in half horizontally*

*1 pound smoked pork shanks,
sliced*

3 sprigs fresh epazote, if desired

*1 pound pinto beans, picked over
& rinsed*

6½ cups water

2 teaspoons coarse salt, or to taste

Heat the lard or oil in a saucepan over medium-high heat and sauté the onion and garlic for 3 to 4 minutes, or until browned. Add the pork, *epazote*, if using, the beans, and water, and bring to a boil. Reduce heat to low and simmer uncovered, stirring occasionally, for about 1 to 1½ hours, or until beans are softened. Remove the onion, garlic, pork, and *epazote*, and add the salt, stirring to combine well. Turn off the heat and let the beans stand, covered, for 15 minutes. This dish can be prepared ahead of time. To reheat, heat beans with ¼ cup water in a saucepan for 5 to 10 minutes, or until heated through, stirring frequently. Makes about 4 to 5 cups. Serves 6.

Basalt figures from a Toltec temple, Tula

FRIJOLES REFRITOS

Refried Beans

Refried beans is one dish that can be a part of almost every meal. To reheat, cook a little more onion in lard over medium heat, then add the beans.

1 recipe Frijoles *(p. 80)*
¼ cup lard or vegetable oil

1 cup chopped white onions
1 teaspoon salt, or to taste

Coarsely mash the beans. Heat the lard or oil in a large skillet over medium-high heat and sauté the onions, for 4 to 5 minutes, or until browned. Add the beans and cook, stirring frequently, for 5 to 8 minutes, or until heated through. Salt to taste. Serves 6.

ENSALADA DE AGUACATE

Avocado Salad

In Mexico, the variety of avocados available is breathtaking to behold.
Some, like those in Oaxaca, are no bigger than large grapes, and are eaten whole,
with skin. Other larger ones hang ponderous from huge trees that drip with the
fruit. It is no wonder that avocados are put to such marvelous culinary
use. This salad is crisp and refreshing, with the pickled onions
adding their unique color and taste.

4 Haas avocados, peeled &
pitted

½ cup coarsely chopped cilantro

⅓ cup chopped white onion

1 cup Chicken Stock (p. 36),
room temperature

1 tablespoon fresh lime juice

1 tablespoon cider vinegar

1½ teaspoons coarse salt, or to
taste

1 large head Romaine lettuce,
outer leaves discarded, inner
leaves separated, rinsed, &
drained

1 bunch watercress, rinsed,
drained, & stemmed

6 ripe plum tomatoes, quartered

Pickled Onions (p. 24) for
garnish

In a blender add 1 avocado, the *cilantro*, onion, stock, juice, vinegar, and salt, and purée until smooth. Transfer dressing to a bowl and cover with plastic wrap.

Cut each of the remaining avocados into eighths. Arrange the lettuce, watercress, tomatoes, and avocados into 6 bowls and garnish with pickled onions. Serve the dressing separately or drizzle over top. Serves 6.

ENSALADA DE NOPALITOS

Nopal Cactus Salad

Who would have even thought that the paddles of the prickly cactus would be edible? They are, and the Mexicans have put them to use in many creative ways. Note that you roast the sliced fresh paddles before tossing them with the other ingredients. Essentially you are drying the cactus out, to remove the sticky substance that is released from the paddles.

2 pounds fresh nopal cactus, or one 28-ounce can sliced cactus in brine, rinsed & drained

⅓ cup or 2 tablespoons olive oil

1 tablespoon or ½ teaspoons coarse salt

1 teaspoon or ¼ teaspoon freshly ground black pepper

4 ripe plum tomatoes, about ½ pound, seeded

¼ pound slivered red onions

4 chiles jalapeños, *stemmed, seeded, ribbed, & thinly sliced lengthwise*

½ cup coarsely chopped cilantro

¼ cup fresh lime juice

Preheat the oven to 450°F.

Carefully hold each fresh cactus paddle, if using, by its base. Cut off thorny nodes with the tip of a sharp paring knife and trim ⅛ inch from around the edge of each leaf. Cut the trimmed paddles into ¼-inch wide strips. Combine cactus strips in a bowl with ⅓ cup oil, 1 tablespoon salt, and 1 teaspoon pepper, and toss to combine. Spread strips in a single layer on 2 large baking pans. Roast for 10 minutes, stir strips to make sure they are not sticking, and roast for another 20 minutes, or until tender. Remove the pans from the oven, and let cool.

Halve the tomatoes vertically, seed, and cut into ⅛-inch strips lengthwise. In a large bowl combine the tomatoes, onions, *chiles, cilantro,* and lime juice. In another bowl

Tower of Santo Domingo Church, Oaxaca

combine the canned cactus, if using, with 2 tablespoons oil, ½ teaspoon salt, and ¼ teaspoon pepper. Add the roasted cactus and oil from the baking pans, or the canned cactus mixture, to tomato mixture, and toss to combine well. Serves 6.

ENSALADA DE JÍCAMA

Jícama Salad

The cool, refreshing crunchiness of *jícama* is well appreciated in Mexico, where it is frequently cut into sticks and served with fresh lime and salt before meals. In this salad, which uses fresh *chiles*, lime juice and a handful of other ingredients, *jícama* stars. Once dressed, the salad should be served immediately, or the red of the radishes will bleed from the acidity of the lime juice.

1 medium jícama, *about 1½ to 2 pounds, peeled & sliced ¼ inch thick*

1 cup slivered white onions

1⅓ cups julienned radishes

5 chiles jalapeños, *stemmed, seeded, ribbed, & thinly sliced lengthwise*

½ cup fresh lime juice

1 tablespoon cider vinegar

2 tablespoons sugar

1 teaspoon coarse salt

⅓ cup vegetable or olive oil

In a large bowl gently toss the *jícama*, onions, radishes, and *chiles*.

In a small bowl whisk together the lime juice, vinegar, sugar, and salt until the sugar is dissolved. Whisk in the oil until combined well. Pour dressing over vegetables and toss to coat. Adjust seasoning, if desired, and serve immediately. Serves 6.

BUÑUELOS

Fritters

These deliciously crisp fritters are *fiesta* food at its finest and are served on holidays and special occasions. The rounds are airy, light, and sweet. When you make them stretch the dough until you can almost see through it. Deep fry them only until delicately brown and serve while they are still warm.

2 cups all-purpose flour

½ teaspoon baking powder

2 tablespoons sugar

1 teaspoon ground canela or ½ teaspoon ground cinnamon

¼ teaspoon coarse salt

1 large egg, beaten

½ cup milk

¼ cup unsalted butter, melted

Vegetable oil for frying

¼ cup sugar

In a large bowl, sift together the flour, baking powder, sugar, *canela*, and salt. In a small bowl, combine the egg, milk, and butter. Add egg mixture to flour mixture and stir until combined and a dough forms. Knead dough on a lightly floured surface for 3 to 4 minutes, or until smooth and elastic, adding more flour if necessary. Cover with plastic and let rest for 15 to 20 minutes. Divide dough into 16 equal balls and cover.

Heat ½ inch oil in a heavy skillet to 370°F. Flatten a ball between your palms and carefully pull the dough into a 4-inch round about ⅛ inch thick. Place into skillet and fry for 1½ to 2 minutes per side, or until crisp and golden. Transfer to paper towels to drain. Repeat with remaining balls. Place 2 or 3 fritters on a dessert plate and sprinkle with sugar. Serve immediately. Makes 16 fritters.

Plátanos Fritos con Miel y Crema & Café de Olla, page 15

PLÁTANOS FRITOS CON MIEL Y CREMA

Fried Plantains with Honey and Cream

The skin of the plantain, a type of banana indigenous to the Caribbean Islands and Mexico, turns pitch black in color when ripe ~ a disarming development if you are accustomed to all that is lost with an overripe regular banana. However, when truly black on the outside, the plantain is ready within, sweet in flavor, but still relatively firm in texture and thus good for cooking. This sweet dessert, typical of the Yucatán, is best prepared in a nonstick skillet, as plantains tend to stick and can burn easily.

½ cup unsalted butter

6 medium plantains, ripened until the skins are blackened, but still firm to the touch

⅓ cup honey for drizzling

½ cup heavy cream, lightly whipped to 1 cup, as an accompaniment

Melt butter in a saucepan over medium-high heat, skimming off scum. Remove from heat and pour clarified butter into a bowl and discard residue left in the pan. Makes ⅓ cup clarified butter.

Peel the plantains and slice them on the diagonal ½ inch thick. Heat 1 scant tablespoon clarified butter in a nonstick skillet over medium heat and brown plantains in batches for about 1 to 1½ minutes per side, or until golden brown. Add butter as needed. Transfer to paper towels to drain.

Divide plantains among dessert plates, drizzle about 1 tablespoon honey over each serving, and serve immediately with whipped cream. Serves 6.

FLAN

Caramel Custard

This sweet, comforting, rich but somehow light dessert is made
throughout Mexico with different flavorings depending on where you are.
Sometimes cinnamon is added; sometimes fruit; in the cities, probably a touch of
liqueur. It will come as no surprise that the combination derives from Spain,
brought to Mexico by Spanish nuns. This is a straightforward rendition of the
custard that bakes in individual molds, with a reasonable, but not overwhelming,
number of eggs. *Flan* is particularly well suited to follow a spicy meal.
Remember to allow enough time for the molds to chill thoroughly.

1¼ cups sugar

¼ cup water

1½ cups milk

1½ cups heavy cream

2 large whole eggs

2 large egg yolks

2 teaspoons pure vanilla extract

Preheat the oven to 350°F. Add 1 cup sugar and the water into a heavy saucepan over medium-high heat and boil until syrup turns a deep golden brown. Remove the pan from the heat and immediately pour equal amounts of syrup into six ½-cup ramekins, tilting cups to distribute syrup evenly on the bottoms and sides.

In a saucepan over medium heat, combine the milk, cream, and remaining sugar. Heat mixture over medium-high until hot, but not boiling. Remove the pan from heat and let mixture cool slightly.

In a small bowl whisk together the eggs and egg yolks until well blended. Slowly pour the eggs into the milk mixture, whisking constantly. Stir in the vanilla

extract. Divide the mixture among the prepared ramekins. Place ramekins in a baking pan and add boiling water to the pan to come about ¾ of the way up the sides of the ramekins. Bake the custards in the water bath for 35 to 45 minutes, or until they no longer tremble when moved. Remove ramekins from the pan, cool, and refrigerate covered for 3 hours. To serve, unmold custards by running a knife around the edge of the ramekins and transfer onto dessert plates. Serves 6.

GLOSSARY OF MEXICAN INGREDIENTS

Canela: This is the name for cinnamon in Mexico, but of the soft, shaggy, and multi-layered sticks of Ceylon cinnamon. Less strong in flavor than the harder regular stick cinnamon used in mulled hot beverages for flavoring, *canela* should be ground in a spice grinder. Store in an airtight container.

Chiles, **Canned:** *Chiles Chipotles en Adobo:* These are smoked *chiles jalapeños* that are then canned in a tomato sauce with vinegar and spices. They add depth, an assertive spiciness, and a wonderful smoky flavor, and can be used chopped or puréed, as in *Chipotle* Puree (p. 70).

Chiles Jalapeños en Escabeche: These are canned *chiles jalapeños* in a vinegar-type liquid. Hot, but not overly so, they add personality and spice. Do not drain off and discard the liquid as it is frequently added to recipes for further heat.

Chiles, **Dried:** *Ancho:* Wrinkled, about 3- to 4-inches long, and relatively wide, *chile ancho* is the *chile poblano* dried. Darkish red, sort of deep burgundy in color, *chiles anchos* are not hot but have a rich, savory, almost sweet flavor. They require soaking before use. Generally available in most well-stocked supermarkets, they should be stored airtight, where they will keep indefinitely.

de Árbol: These long, thin, tapered *chiles* are orangey to deep red when dried and they are very hot. Before using, they are soaked in water to cover or are toasted. Keep in an airtight container in a dry place.

Guajillo: This dried *chile* may be more difficult to find. It is tapered, about 3½- to 4½-inches long and 1-inch wide. It is reddish brown in color and is pleasantly hot, but not fiery. Will need soaking before use. Keep in an airtight container in a dry place.

Mulato: Called for with two other different *chiles* in *Mole Poblano de Guajolote* (p. 63), *chiles mulatos* are about half as wide as they are long, and slightly resemble the shape of a bell pepper. Brownish red in color, they are similar to the *chile ancho* in shape but different in flavor. The *mulato* has a medium hot, nonsweet taste. Keep in an airtight container in a dry place.

Pasilla: This dark, almost black, *chile* has an earthy, tobacco-like flavor. It is long and narrow, about 4- to 6-inches long, ¾- to 1-inch wide, and its skin is wrinkled. Keep in an airtight container in a dry place.

Chiles, **Fresh:** Among the profusion of fresh green *chiles* grown in Mexico, the ones that follow are probably the best known outside of Mexico's borders. And while descriptions of *chiles* are useful and will serve as a good introduction to their basic characteristics, there is no substitute for buying them, preparing them, and tasting them. In so doing, you will learn what is meant by hot but not fiery, savory, or mild. You will also be able to judge just the amount to use to satisfy your own personal tastes. If you are making a dish for the first time and there is a range of fresh *chiles* called for in the recipe, it is a good idea to incorporate the smallest amount. You can then add to that. Once incorporated into a preparation, the power of a fresh *chile* cannot be removed.

When handling fresh *chiles,* we recommend that you wear gloves. Prepare the *chiles* as suggested in the recipe, beginning with

removing the stems. Halve the *chiles,* remembering that the seeds and the ribs are what carry the most heat. (If you like a peppery effect, use the seeds. Otherwise discard them.) While preparing *chiles,* do not touch your eyes or nose, as the pepper will cause a very real burning sensation. Rinse the gloves after preparing the *chiles.*

Jalapeño: About 1-inch wide and 2-inches long, this medium to dark green *chile* is readily available in supermarkets. It ranges from hot to very hot depending on the season and is called for frequently in recipes. The *chile serrano* is a reasonable substitute. Store in a plastic bag in the refrigerator.

Poblano: This is the fresh *chile* that when dried becomes the *ancho.* Dark green in color, about 2-inches wide and 3- to 4-inches long, and sort of heart-shaped, it ranges from medium to hot in taste. Store in a plastic bag

in the refrigerator.

Serrano: This *chile,* so often used as a substitute for the *jalapeño,* is very tapered and thinner by comparison to the *jalapeño.* It can be bright or dark green and is spirited in flavor and usually very hot in taste. It adds personality and punch to salsas and dips. Store in a plastic bag in the refrigerator.

Chocolate, Mexican: Available in 3-ounce tablets, this sweet chocolate has had ground almonds, cinnamon, and vanilla added. Store in an airtight container at room temperature. If unavailable, substitute semi-sweet or extra-bittersweet chocolate, which will be less sweet and untextured.

Cilantro: This fresh herb, which also goes by the names coriander or Chinese parsley, is sold in bunches of sprigs with leaves that resemble those of flat-leaf parsley. *Cilantro* is strong, some would call it powerful, in flavor, and you may want to use less of it should you be new to its distinct taste. Store in the refrigerator in a plastic bag. Do not use if tinged with yellow; *cilantro* past its prime has an unpleasant odor and taste.

Condimento de Achiote: A paste the consistency of modeling clay that is made from ground *annatto* seeds, *chiles*, and spices. It is savory, but not overpowering. Sold in 3-ounce or larger packages. Store opened packages, wrapped, in the refrigerator.

Corn Husks, Dried: Available in 8-ounce packages, the dried husks from fresh ears of corn require soaking before use as wrappers in *Tamales con Puerco y Chile Rojo* (p. 30). The husks are not edible. Will keep indefinitely, wrapped and stored in a dry place.

Epazote: This herb, which grows wild in Mexico and in many parts of North America, is at its best fresh. Its flavor is unique, strong, and not necessarily to each person's liking on account of its pungency. The fresh leaves are spiky and green. Some maintain that there is no substitute for *epazote*.

Masa; Masa Harina: *Masa* is corn dough made from corn that has been cooked in lime ~ not the citrus fruit but the mineral ~ and water, then ground fine. In Mexico, near tortilla factories, fresh *masa* can actually be bought, but it is highly perishable; the answer, it would seem, for foreigners and Mexicans alike, could well be the dried substitute, *masa harina*. The main ingredient in corn tortillas, *masa harina* is readily available under the Quaker brand in many supermarkets. Neither regular cornmeal nor corn flour can be used as a replacement.

Pepitas: This is the word in Mexico for pumpkin seeds. They are sold unsalted and shelled in packages, are green in color, and lend texture and a subtle nutty flavor to sauces, or *moles*, such in *Pollo en Pipián Verde* (p. 61). They can also be eaten as snacks.

Pozole: These lime-treated dried corn kernels, or hominy, are available in packages, and are used for making one of the most famous dishes of Mexico, *pozole*. Chewy and puffed when cooked, the dried variety of *pozole* should first be soaked for a minimum of 8 hours before use. Whole hominy in cans, drained then rinsed, can be substituted, but with considerably less toothsome results.

Queso: *Añejo:* This is aged Mexican white cheese, slightly acidic and salty, that is used, crumbled, in such renowned dishes as *Enchiladas Suizas* (p. 56). Store, wrapped airtight, in the refrigerator. A reasonable substitute is the Greek cheese, feta, crumbled, although it is probably somewhat saltier by comparison.

Fresco: This is fresh Mexican white cheese that is bland in flavor and used crumbled in fillings in such dishes as *Enchiladas Rojas con Queso* (p. 58). Monterey Jack cheese, grated, can be substituted.

Salt, Coarse: For the recipes in this book, coarse, large-grained salt has been used for its subtle seasoning power. If you are used to using regular iodized salt, do not use an equivalent amount of coarse salt, because the dish will be oversalted and inedible.

WEIGHTS

OUNCES AND POUNDS	METRICS
¼ ounce	7 grams
⅓ ounce	10 grams
½ ounce	14 grams
1 ounce	28 grams
1¾ ounces	50 grams
2 ounces	57 grams
2⅔ ounces	75 grams
3 ounces	85 grams
3½ ounces	100 grams
4 ounces (¼ pound)	114 grams
6 ounces	170 grams
8 ounces (½ pound)	227 grams
9 ounces	250 grams
16 ounces (1 pound)	464 grams
1.1 pounds	500 grams
2.2 pounds	1,000 grams (1 kilogram)

TEMPERATURES

°F (FAHRENHEIT)	°C (CENTIGRADE OR CELSIUS)
32 (water freezes)	0
108-110 (warm)	42-43
140	60
203 (water simmers)	95
212 (water boils)	100
225 (very slow oven)	107.2
245	120
266	130
300 (slow oven)	149
350 (moderate oven)	177
375	191
400 (hot oven)	205
450	232
500 (very hot oven)	260

LIQUID MEASURES

tsp.: teaspoon
Tbs.: tablespoon

SPOONS AND CUPS	METRIC EQUIVALENTS
1 tsp.	5 milliliters (5 grams)
2 tsp.	10 milliliters (10 grams)
3 tsp. (1 Tbs.)	15 milliliters (15 grams)
3⅓ Tbs.	½ deciliter (50 milliliters)
¼ cup	59 milliliters
⅓ cup	1 deciliter less 1⅓ Tbs.
⅓ cup + 1 Tbs.	1 deciliter (100 milliliters)
1 cup	¼ liter less 1¼ Tbs.
1 cup + 1¼ Tbs.	¼ liter
2 cups	½ liter less 2½ Tbs.
2 cups + 2½ Tbs.	½ liter
4 cups	1 liter less 1 deciliter
4⅓ cups + 1 Tbs.	1 liter (1,000 milliliters)

INDEX